MUSIC RIGHTS
The Venture Class

CONTENTS

MUSIC RIGHTS

REVENUE SHARING AND MUSIC RIGHTS LEASE AGREEMENT FINAL DRAFT

        THIS REVENUE SHARING AND MUSIC RIGHTS LEASE AGREEMENT ("AGREEMENT" or "REVENUE SHARING LEASE AGREEMENT") is dated MM/DD/YYYY and entered into by and between

_____., ("Seller") a Individual having its principal residence at _____, _____, ___, _____ - _____ and

_____, ("Investor"), a individual/corporation, having its office and place of business at _____, _____, ___, _____ - _____

MUSIC RIGHTS

IN CONSIDERATION of the mutual agreements set forth hereinafter,
the parties agree as follows:

    1. LEASED RIGHTS. This Agreement and each Music Rights Schedule (as
defined below) entered into under this Agreement shall describe the
Intellectual property leased under this Agreement and shall be subject to all
terms and conditions hereunder. Each Music Rights Schedule to be entered into
between _____ and Purchaser pursuant to this Agreement shall be
in the form annexed hereto as Attachment I (the "MUSIC RIGHTS SCHEDULE").
Each Music Rights Schedule shall be enforceable according to the terms and
conditions contained therein and such terms and conditions are incorporated
into this Agreement. Capitalized terms not otherwise defined in this
Agreement shall have the meanings ascribed to such terms in each Music Rights
Schedule. In the event of a conflict between the terms of this Agreement and
any Music Rights Schedule, the terms of the Music Rights Schedule shall
prevail with respect to that Music Rights Schedule.

    Seller agrees to place with Purchaser, and Purchaser agrees to
accept and lease from Seller, in accordance with the terms and conditions
herein, the Music Rights and features together with all trading privileges,
and SUB RIGHTS related thereto (collectively referred to as the "MUSIC
RIGHTS" and individually as a ("MUSIC RIGHT") described in each executed
Music Rights Schedule. Purchaser shall have no right, title or interest in
the Music Rights, except as expressly set forth in this Agreement. Seller and
Purchaser shall have no obligation hereunder until the execution and delivery
of an Music Rights Schedule by Seller and Purchaser. Purchaser agrees that
Seller will be the exclusive provider of the Music Rights and has verified
obtaining a valid MIME Music Investment Market Exchange) official market
identifier for the QMS (Qualified Matching Service) BBS published prices
authorized in March 2012 International Standard Serial Number DIGICIRC, and
has a valid and current associate national QMS membership for reporting
requirements by the Exempt Commodity Pool Operator NFA (National Futures
Association) ID 0436761 during the term of this Agreement.

Music Investment and Market Exchange
Official market identifier for the
national QMS (Qualified Matching
Service) BBS published prices

DIGICIRC

MEMORANDUM

Real sample data
2013 Anticipated Re-launch
Test, Non-Adjusted
Trailing Prices.

M R	National QMS ID	M R Units	M R S	Value	Sales	Unit Price
213	MRQMS2005106X213	1	100	$1.00	N/A	$0.01
901	MRQMS2005106X901	1	100	$1.00	0.65	$0.01
619	MRQMS2005106X619	1	100	$1.00	1.30	$0.01
505	MRQMS2005106X505	1	100	$1.00	0.65	$0.01
406	MRQMS2005106X406	1	100	$1.00	0.60	$0.01

All M R data provided initial minimum Book value **of** $0.0001.
NFA (National Futures Association) ID 0436761

ISSN
2166-711X
Issue Price
2.99

National QMS Authorized Publisher
JMGT Studios Satellite Television Network LLC

Address
7485 SVL Box
Victorville, CA 92395

Authentic Representation

M R

(MUSIC RIGHTS)
CERTIFICATE NUMBER
UNITS

Sample Specimen

Authorized Certificate of Units

CERTIFIES the owner of the Unit representing the total M R minimum Book value $0.0001 U.S.D per M R of undivided interest. A certified Music Right, BMI, ASCAP, and Sound scan authorized encoding. Units held by the Members are reflected in the electronic Certificate Register of the Company.

IN WITNESS WHEREOF, the Company has authorized Certificates to be signed by its authorized signatory for the year of 2012. The Authorized M R Certificate of Units is not a part of any Copyright pools under NFA (National Futures Association) ID 0436761, and is certified to exist apart from such exempt commodity pool(s) in Operation and is not authorized to be included in such commodity pool(s), unless issued as a part of an authorized commodity pool.

Certified Authentication

Differs from Authorized certificate of Units above and are distributed only by the Authorized Publisher/Provider unless otherwise noted on the MIME Music Investment and Market Exchange Official market identifier for the national QMS (Qualified Matching Service) BBS published prices.

Questions

For questions regarding the publisher, content, or published prices please contact or write to:

JMGT Studios Satellite Television Network LLC
7485 SVL Box Victorville, CA 92395

2. TERM: PAYMENTS AND TERMINATION. The term ("TERM") of this Agreement shall commence on the date set forth above and shall continue thereafter so long as any Music Rights Schedule entered into pursuant to this Agreement remains in effect.

The lease term and lease payment for the Music Right shall be as stated herein and in the respective Music Rights Schedule(s). At the end of such lease term provided no Event of Default (as hereinafter defined) has occurred and is continuing, Purchaser shall not have the exercisable option to the Seller for (A) purchasing the Music Rights for its then Fair Market Value (as hereinafter defined), (B) renew the Music Rights Schedule(s) under mutually acceptable terms through the national QMS provided service, or (C) terminate the Music Rights Schedule(s) according to its terms.

Payments in the full amount required to exercise unauthorized Purchaser's option to purchase the Music Rights, shall be deemed null and void and without effect, and no transfer of rights, title and interest in the Music Rights to unauthorized Purchasers regardless of any express or implied representations or warranties whatsoever concerning the purchase of the Music Rights in its entirety.

If, upon the termination of the applicable Music Rights Schedule as to any perceived MUSIC RIGHTS ITEMS, Purchaser fails or refuses to return and deliver possession of MUSIC RIGHTS to Seller pursuant to Section 15 hereof within zero (0) business days after the expiration of the term of the Music Rights Schedule, in addition to all other rights and remedies available to Seller, Purchaser shall be liable to Seller for the Fair Market Value of such MUSIC RIGHT until returned to Seller as well as all other damages incurred by Seller.

All Payments (as hereinafter defined) shall, unless otherwise directed by the price publisher in writing, be made to Seller on the Payment Date (as hereinafter defined) by electronic transfer of funds, and Purchaser shall execute all authorizations necessary for such electronic transfers. If the Payment Date is not a business day, Payments for such period shall be due on the next business day. Any Payment not made by the related Payment Date shall be subject to a late payment fee of one percent (1%) of the outstanding Payment amount.

3. ACCEPTANCE, WARRANTIES AND LIMITATION OF LIABILITY. Purchaser shall execute and deliver to price publisher an authorized and signed certificate of acceptance (the "CERTIFICATE") available from the price publisher the authorized Music Rights Schedule with respect to each MUSIC RIGHT and NO MUSIC RIGHTS ITEMS available from the SELLER, UNLESS APPENDED TO THE AUTHORIZED MUSIC RIGHT AS A MUSIC RIGHTS ITEM and acknowledge the acceptance of each such MUSIC RIGHT and each MUSIC RIGHTS ITEM. Purchaser represents and agrees that, as of the date each MUSIC RIGHT and or MUSIC RIGHTS ITEM is accepted pursuant to a Certificate (the "ACCEPTANCE DATE"), such Certificate shall be conclusive evidence that each MUSIC RIGHT and each MUSIC RIGHTS ITEM is authentic in size, design, trade ability, unit capacity and manufacture by the price publisher and that Purchaser has inspected each such MUSIC RIGHT and each MUSIC RIGHTS ITEM, found it to be in good order, and unconditionally accepts such MUSIC RIGHT and or each MUSIC RIGHTS ITEM(s), subject to any right or remedy Purchaser may have against the manufacturer or supplier thereof. Notwithstanding any relationship between Seller and the price publisher, supplier or Servicer of the Music Rights, Seller shall have no liability to Purchaser for any claim, loss or damage caused or alleged to be caused directly, indirectly, incidentally or consequentially by the Music Rights, by any inadequacy or deficiency thereof or, defect therein, by any incident whatsoever in connection therewith, or in any way related to or arising out of this Agreement whether arising in contract, strict liability, negligence or otherwise. Purchaser shall not assert any claims, counterclaims, or defenses against the price publisher, Seller for consequential, special or indirect damages, or for loss of use or loss of profits. The price publisher and Seller makes no express or implied warranties of any kind, including those of merchantability, durability, or fitness for a particular purpose or use with respect
to the Music Rights and expressly disclaims the same.

4

4. ASSIGNMENT, OBLIGATION TO MAKE PAYMENTS UNCONDITIONAL. Seller may Not assign or sell all or a portion of its Music Rights title, and Music Rights interest in, or any MUSIC RIGHTS ITEM appended to this authorized Music Rights, in this Agreement, and/or any Music Rights Schedule, and/or grant a security interest in the Music Rights, or any MUSIC RIGHTS ITEMS appended to the authorized Music Rights, in this Agreement, and/or any Music Rights Schedule, to any third party (hereinafter, "ASSIGNEE"). Any such assignment as required by law or sale required by law shall not relieve Seller or ASSIGNEE of any of its obligations hereunder. Purchaser hereby: (A) consents to such sales, assignments and/or grants; (B) agrees to execute promptly and deliver such further acknowledgments, agreements and other instruments as may be reasonably requested by the price publisher, or any Assignee to effect such assignments and/or grants; and (C) agrees to comply fully with the terms of any such assignments and/or grants. In the event of an assignment, Assignee shall have all rights and benefits of Seller under this Agreement, but Assignee shall not be obligated to perform the obligations of Seller hereunder unless Assignee expressly agrees to do so in writing. Purchaser and Seller or ASSIGNEE agrees that its obligation to pay all Payments and other sums payable hereunder and the rights of Purchaser, Seller and Assignee in and to such Payments, are absolute and unconditional and are not subject to any abatement, reduction, set off, defense, counterclaim or

recoupment due or alleged to be due, to or by reason of, any past, present or future claims which Seller, ASSIGNEE, Purchaser may have against them. Purchaser shall have the right to assign this Agreement, any Music Rights Schedule, or to Sublease the Music Rights without the express prior written consent of Seller, which consent shall not

be unreasonably withheld, by obtaining a valid MIME Music Investment Market Exchange) official market identifier for the QMS (Qualified Matching Service) BBS published prices during a valid and current Seller, ASSIGNEE associate national QMS membership for reporting requirements by the Exempt Commodity Pool Operator NFA (National Futures Association) ID 0436761 during the term of this Agreement.

By obtaining an authorized listing of the Sub Lease Rights. Purchaser agree to the terms and conditions of any Sublease of the Music Rights as outlined by the MIME Music Investment Market Exchange Official market policies for assigning Music Rights on the national QMS (Qualified Matching Service) BBS.

Sub Rights Policy

Purchaser shall have the right to assign this Agreement, any Music Rights Schedule, as a Sublease to the Music Rights without regard to published prices, and any Revenues attributed to the Music Rights. The Sub Rights Policy referenced herein is incorporate into the entire Sub Rights Policy available on the MIME Music Investment Market Exchange Official market policies and Guideline for assigning Music Rights posted on the national QMS (Qualified Matching Service) BBS.

     5. ASSOCIATE MEMBERSHIP. Seller, ASSIGNEES at its expense, shall be responsible for the associate membership fees, while a member of the MIME Music Investment Market Exchange national QMS (Qualified Matching Service) BBS for the Music Rights and Sub Rights, all of which shall be effected by the Servicer (defined in this paragraph) or such other third party as authorized and acceptable by to price publisher.

5
Seller agrees, at all times during the Term, at its sole expense, to keep the Music Rights in good repair, condition and working order, and to furnish all reports which may be required in the course of so doing. Purchaser shall at all times during the Term, refrain from Co-Maintenance practices notwithstanding generally accepted social media texting in outlets, covering the Music Rights and or Sub Rights and or such other professional third party marketing as may be acceptable to Seller (any such party, the "SERVICER").

Seller or Assignee will have the right, but not the obligation, to inspect the Music Rights during reasonable business hours directly with the Qualified Matching Service not including scheduled pre-live dates. As a material inducement for Purchaser to enter into this Agreement with Seller on a "revenue sharing basis" Seller shall:

(A) Purchase and maintain a membership, so as to maximize the revenue generating capability of the Music Rights;

(B) Take all actions and pay all costs necessary to cause the MUSIC RIGHTS and MUSIC RIGHTS ITEMS to transfer to the Purchaser;

(C) Perform all of the above obligations in a manner satisfactory to the Qualified Matching Service.

6. REPRESENTATIONS AND WARRANTIES. Seller represents and warrants for the benefit of Purchaser and any Assignee (as hereinafter defined) and if requested by Purchaser will provide an unqualified and or qualified opinion of counsel and other supporting documents reasonably requested by Purchaser to the effect that, at the time of execution of this Agreement and of each Music Rights Schedule:

(A) Seller is an individual authorized to enter into a binding agreement, or a legal entity, or duly organized, validly existing and in good standing under the law of the jurisdiction where the Music Rights will be located and has adequate power to enter into and perform this Agreement and each Music Rights Schedule executed hereinafter;

(B) This Agreement and each Music Rights Schedule and Maintenance Agreement executed hereinafter has been duly authorized, executed and delivered by Seller and together constitute a valid, legal and binding agreement of Purchaser, each enforceable in accordance with its terms;

(C) The entering into and performance of this Agreement and each Music Rights Schedule executed hereinafter will not violate any provision of Seller's articles of incorporation or bylaws, and to the best of Seller's knowledge, will not violate any judgment, order, or result in any breach of, or constitute a default under, or result in the creation of any lien, charge, security interest or other encumbrance upon any assets of Seller or on the Music Rights of this Agreement pursuant to any instrument to which Seller is a party or by which it or its assets may be bound pursuant to any law or regulation applicable to Seller;

6

(D) To the best of Seller's knowledge there are no actions, suits or proceedings pending or, threatened, before any court, administrative agency, arbitrator or government body which will, if determined adversely to Seller, materially adversely affect its ability to perform its obligations under this Agreement, or Music Rights Schedule, executed hereinafter or any related agreement to which Seller is a party;

(E) That all financial reports and information and other information furnished in connection with this Agreement was, at the time of delivery, true and correct in all respects.

7. RISK OF LOSS AND DAMAGE.

(A) Seller, ASSIGNEES agrees to bear the entire risk of loss with respect to any damage, destruction, loss, or theft of the Music Rights and any MUSIC RIGHTS ITEMS, whether insured or not, whether such loss is partial or complete and from any cause at all, whether or not through any default or neglect of Seller, ASSIGNEE (except if such damage, destruction, loss or theft arises from the gross negligence or willful misconduct of Seller, ASSIGNEE) from the Acceptance Date, until the expiration date of such MUSIC RIGHTS and MUSIC RIGHTS ITEM or zero (0) days after such MUSIC RIGHTS and or MUSIC RIGHTS ITEMS are returned pursuant to Section 15 hereof. Except as provided in this Section 7, no such event shall relieve Seller of its obligation to make Payments hereunder.

(B) If any MUSIC RIGHTS or MUSIC RIGHTS ITEMS is damaged and capable of repair, Seller must promptly notify the Company and within twenty four (24) hours of such damage shall, at Seller's expense, cause such repairs to be made as are necessary to return such MUSIC RIGHTS and or MUSIC RIGHTS ITEMS to its condition prior to such damage. This is termed the New CREDITS period.

(C) In the event any MUSIC RIGHT or MUSIC RIGHTS ITEMS is destroyed, damaged beyond repair, lost or stolen, (an "EVENT OF LOSS"), Seller must promptly notify the Company and Assignee and pay to Purchaser or Assignee, as the case may be, on the first Payment Date following the Event of Loss, a discount amount equal to the MUSIC RIGHTS or MUSIC RIGHTS ITEMS book value in the form of a credit Price which will be reflected as an price or credit to the published price (as defined in the relevant Music Rights Schedule) and all Payments accrued on any such MUSIC RIGHTS or MUSIC RIGHTS ITEMS during the time the MUSIC RIGHTS or MUSIC RIGHTS items were not trading (or during the New Credits period). Upon payment of such amounts in full, Seller's obligation to pay any further Payments will cease with respect to such MUSIC RIGHTS ITEM(s) (but not with respect to any of the remaining Music Rights) and Purchaser will be entitled to receive any insurance proceeds or other recovery received by Seller or Assignee in connection with such Event of Loss.

7

8. INSURANCE. Seller, at its sole expense, shall insure the Music Rights and MUSIC RIGHTS ITEMS (at their own discretion) against all risks and in such amounts as Seller reasonably requires (but not less than the "spin price" or issue price) or initial published price, as defined in the relevant Music Rights Schedule), of all MUSIC RIGHTS and MUSIC RIGHTS ITEMS set forth in the Music Rights Schedule(s) with insurance carrier(s) acceptable to Seller and shall maintain a loss payable endorsement in favor of Seller and Assignee affording them such additional protection as they reasonably require; and shall maintain

liability insurance reasonably (at their own discretion) satisfactory to Seller. Such insurance policies shall insure against, among other exposures, property damage liabilities, and other risks customarily insured against by Seller on MUSIC RIGHTS and MUSIC RIGHTS ITEMS owned by Seller. All such insurance policies must name Seller, and Assignee as insured and loss payees. Each insurer is hereby authorized and directed to make payment for any Loss directly to Seller or Assignee. If Seller, ASSIGNEE does not provide evidence of insurance acceptable to Seller or Assignees, Seller has the right, but not the obligation, to obtain insurance covering the Music Rights from an insurer of Seller's choice. Seller may add the costs of acquiring and maintaining such insurance and all fees in placing and maintaining such insurance (collectively, "INSURANCE CHARGE") to the Pre-Purchase or Pre-Issue price prior to a live listing, which may delay the listing date. Nothing in this Agreement will create an insurance relationship of any type between Seller or Assignee, and any other person. Purchaser acknowledges that Seller and Assignee are not required to secure or maintain any insurance, and Seller and Assignee will not be liable to Purchaser or anyone else if Seller or Assignee terminate any insurance coverage that Seller or Assignee procure, unless such cancellation is during the live period. In the event of such a cancellation the Purchaser will enter a **new Debits** period.

Seller must promptly notify the Company and Assignee and pay to Purchaser or Assignee, as the case may be, on the first Payment Date following the Event of an cancellation of insurance, an increased amount equal to the MUSIC RIGHTS or MUSIC RIGHTS ITEMS book value in the form of a debit Price which will be reflected as an price or debit to the published price (as defined in the relevant Music Rights Schedule) during the duration of the trading time the MUSIC RIGHTS or MUSIC RIGHTS items were not covered with insurance (or during the New Debits period). Upon payment of such amounts in full, Seller's obligation to pay any further Payments will cease with respect to such MUSIC RIGHTS and MUSIC RIGHTS ITEMS.

If Seller or Assignee agree to renew any insurance coverage notwithstanding any actual renewals, Seller or Assignee will not issue New Debits to the Purchaser.

8

9. INDEMNITY. Purchaser agrees to indemnify, hold harmless and defend, Seller, Assignee and Servicer (if applicable) and any of their officers, directors or employees and their successors and assigns (all such parties the "INDEMNIFIED PARTIES")from and against any and all claims, demands, actions, suits, proceedings, costs, expenses, damages and liabilities, at law or in equity, whether based on a theory of contract, negligence, strict liability or otherwise, including reasonable attorneys' fees related thereto, arising out of, connected with, or resulting from, this Agreement, any Music Rights Schedule executed hereunder, the Maintenance Agreement or the Music Rights, including without limitation, the manufacture, selection, purchase, delivery, possession, condition, use, lease, operation or return thereof, or any defects in the Music Rights, except to the extent a claim has arisen from such Indemnified Party's own

gross negligence or willful misconduct (as opposed to any vicarious liability). Purchaser's obligations hereunder will survive the expiration of this Agreement with respect to acts or events occurring or alleged to have occurred prior to the return of the Music Rights to Seller at the end of the Term.

10. LIENS AND TAXES. Seller owns and holds title to the Music copyright(s). Purchaser owns and holds title to the Music Rights and Lease Agreement. Purchaser will, at its sole expense, keep the Music Rights free and clear of all levies, liens and encumbrances. Purchaser will declare and pay to the appropriate governmental authorities when due all license fees, registration fees, assessments, charges and taxes, whether municipal, state or federal (foreign and domestic), including but not limited to, sales and excise taxes, and penalties and interest with respect thereto, excluding, however, any use or property taxes or any taxes measured solely by Purchaser's net income. Seller shall provide evidence of any payment hereunder upon request of authorized governmental agencies. Purchaser's obligations hereunder will survive the expiration of this Agreement with respect to liens or taxes accruing or attaching or alleged to have accrued or attached prior to the return of the Music Rights and or MUSIC RIGHTS ITEMS to Seller at the end of the term of the applicable Music Rights Schedule(s).

11. PURCHASER'S FAILURE TO PERFORM. After the occurrence of an Event of Default (as hereinafter described), Seller has the right, but not the obligation, and without releasing Purchaser from any obligation hereunder, to make or do the same, to pay, purchase, contest or compromise any encumbrance, charge or lien which, in the reasonable judgment of Seller, appears to affect the Music Rights or this Agreement and, in exercising any such rights, incur any liability and expend whatever amount in Seller's reasonable discretion Seller may deem necessary therefor not to exceed 1% of the initial book value of the MUSIC RIGHTS and MUSIC RIGHTS ITEMS. All sums so incurred or expended by Seller shall be, without demand, immediately due and payable by Purchaser, shall be considered Payments hereunder, and will not bear interest monthly and will be credited to the list price as NEW CREDITS.

9

12. MUSIC RIGHTS and MUSIC RIGHTS ITEMS IS PERSONAL PROPERTY; LOCATION OF MUSIC RIGHTS. Purchaser covenants and agrees that the Music copyrights and Music rights Items is, and will at all times be and remain, personal property of Seller or Assignee. If requested by Seller, Purchaser will obtain, prior to delivery of any MUSIC RIGHTS and MUSIC RIGHTS ITEMS, electronic verification in a form satisfactory to the Company from all parties with an interest in the Premises wherein the Music Rights and Music Rights Items may be located, waiving any claim with respect to the Music Rights and other items reasonably requested by the Company. All data and information collected by the Company, at all times during the term and thereinafter, is the property of the Company.

13. DESIGNATION OF MUSIC RIGHTS AND MUSIC RIGHTS ITEMS OWNERSHIP.

If at any time during the term hereof, Seller is supplied with labels, plates or other markings stating that the Music Rights and Music Rights Items is owned by Seller or is subject to any interest of Assignee, Seller agrees to affix and keep the same displayed on the Music Rights and Music rights Items; provided however, that such placement shall not be obtrusive to the Purchaser or users of the Music Rights and Music Rights Items while leased by the Purchaser. Purchaser agrees that this Agreement is a true lease. However, as a precaution in the event (and only to the extent) the transactions underlying this Agreement are deemed to be a lease intended for security, Purchaser, hereby grants Seller and Assigns a first priority purchase money security interest in the Music Rights and Music Rights

Items. Seller agrees to execute and file Uniform Commercial Code financing statements with the Purchasers pre authorized permission, with NEW CREDITS reflected in the listed price and any and all other instruments necessary to perfect (in Seller's opinion) Seller's or Assignee's music copyright interest (as applicable). The Purchaser additionally will be named as a secured party in the Chattel paper only and any Music Rights Schedule(s), the Music Rights and Music rights Items or the payments due hereunder and shall not affect the copyright tile in any manner. Seller may file a copy of this Agreement and appropriate Music Rights Schedule(s) as a financing statement. A Purchaser causing the seller to file a Uniform Commercial Code financing statements a discount amount equal to the MUSIC RIGHTS or MUSIC RIGHTS ITEMS book value in the form of a credit Price which will be reflected as an price or credit to the published price (as defined in the relevant Music Rights Schedule)

14. USE. Purchaser shall use the Music Rights in a careful and proper manner in conformance with Seller's, manufacturer's, supplier's and Servicer's specifications and shall comply with, and conform to, all federal, state, municipal and other laws, ordinances and regulations in any way relating to the possession, use or maintenance of the Music Rights and Music Rights Items.

10

15. SURRENDER OF MUSIC RIGHTS AND MUSIC RIGHTS ITEMS. Upon the expiration or earlier termination of each Music Rights Schedule with respect to any MUSIC RIGHTS AND MUSIC RIGHTS ITEMS, Seller shall: (A)make all Payments due to Purchaser through and including such termination or expiration date; and (B) Purchaser shall return the same to Seller in good repair, condition and working order unless Purchaser has paid Seller in cash the Fair Market Value of the Music Rights and Music Rights Items. Such return shall be effected promptly automatic expiration by making the Music Rights and Music rights Items available to Seller or such other party designated by Seller. Upon return, all components of the Music Rights and Music Rights Items shall be immediately available for sale.

The Sub Lease of the Music Rights and Sub Music Rights Items shall be done in a manner resulting in no harm or damage to the Music Rights and Music Rights Items. All the arrangements for (A) the transportation of each MUSIC RIGHT and each MUSIC RIGHTS ITEMS to and the Sub Lease of each MUSIC RIGHT and

SUB MUSIC RIGHTS ITEMS at the Music Rights location stated in the applicable Music Rights Schedule, and (B) the expiration, and transportation of each SUB MUSIC RIGHT and SUB MUSIC RIGHTS ITEMS from the Sub Music Rights location to a location of Seller's choice within the United States upon the termination of the applicable Music Rights Schedule (by expiration or otherwise) as to such Placed Item. No costs shall be incurred of expiration and transportation of the Music Rights.

16. DEFAULT. The occurrence of any of the following events shall constitute an event of default ("EVENT OF DEFAULT"): (A) failure of Purchaser to receive any Payment on the date on which it is due which failure is not cured within five (5) calendar days after notice thereof from Purchaser (B) failure by Seller to perform or observe any other term, covenant or condition of this Agreement, any Music Rights Schedule, which is not cured within thirty (5) calendar days after notice thereof from Purchaser; (C) any affirmative act of insolvency by Seller, or the filing by Seller of any petition or action under any bankruptcy, reorganization, insolvency arrangement, liquidation dissolution or moratorium law, or any other law or laws for the relief of, or relating to debtors; (D) the filing of any involuntary petition against Seller under any bankruptcy, reorganization, insolvency arrangement, liquidation, dissolution or moratorium law for the relief of or relating to debtors which is not dismissed within sixty (60) days thereafter, or the appointment of any receiver, liquidator or trustee to take possession of any substantial portion of the properties of Purchaser, unless the appointment is set aside or ceases to be in
effect within sixty (60) days from the date of said filing or appointment; (E) the subjection of a substantial part of Seller's EC property or any MUSIC RIGHTS and MUSIC RIGHTS ITEMS to any levy, seizure, assignment or sale for or by any creditor or governmental agency; (F) any representation or warranty made by Purchaser in this Agreement or in any Music Rights Schedule or in any document furnished by Seller to Purchaser or Assignee in connection with this Agreement or any Music Rights Schedule or with respect to the acquisition or use of the Music Rights and Music rights Items shall be untrue in any material respect at any time; (G) the default by Seller under any other lease or loan agreement which materially and/or adversely affects Purchaser's ability to perform its obligations under this Agreement; or (H) if any MUSIC RIGHTS and MUSIC RIGHTS ITEMS is sold or has a lien or encumbrance placed upon it by someone other than Purchaser or Assignee.

11

17. REMEDIES. Upon the occurrence of an Event of Default, Purchaser may do one or more of the following:

(A) Require Seller, ASSIGNEE, upon demand of Purchaser, on the next Payment Date following such demand, pay Purchaser, as liquidated damages and not as a penalty, an amount equal to the Liquidated Damage Value (as set forth in Attachment II hereto), multiplied by 2x the Music Rights book value, together with any Payments then due and owing by Purchaser hereunder, without any costs and expenses owed under this Agreement, not including commissions incurred by Purchaser as a result of an Event of Default and the exercise of Purchaser's remedies with respect thereto (all such amounts collectively the "DEFAULT VALUE"), without interest on the Default Value.

(B) Seller (or its representative) may, without notice to or demand upon Purchaser, take possession of the Music Rights and Sub lease and/or sell the same, or any portion thereof, in such manner or amount, and to such entity as Seller, in Seller's discretion by calling the MUSIC RIGHTS and MUSIC RIGHTS ITEMS. If Seller elects to sell or lease the Music Rights, Seller may do so at a public or private sale or lease by notifying the MIME Music Investment market and exchange and upon notice to Purchaser, which notice will be deemed to be commercially reasonable if the time and place of any public sale, lease or other intended disposition or the time after which any private sale, lease or other intended disposition is to be made shall be sent by authorized electronic communication, to Purchaser no later than ten (10) days prior to such proposed sale, lease or other disposition. The proceeds of such sale or lease will be applied by Seller (i) first, to pay Purchaser an amount equal to the Default book value; and (ii) second, to give the Purchaser First right of Refusal on a Sub Music Rights or Sub Music Rights Items the Purchaser chooses, with an increased amount equal to the MUSIC RIGHTS or MUSIC RIGHTS ITEMS book value that was called credited to the SUB MUSIC RIGHT lease book value plus a DEBIT To The new MUSIC RIGHTS and MUSIC RIGHTS ITEMS in the form of a debit Price which will be reflected as an price or debit to the New MUSIC RIGHTS and MUSIC RGHTS ITEMS published price (as defined in the relevant Music Rights Schedule) during the first day of the trading time to the MUSIC RIGHTS or MUSIC RIGHTS items in an amount equal to the Default book value.

18. MISCELLANEOUS.

(A) EFFECT OF WAIVER. No delay or omission to exercise any right or remedy accruing to Purchaser upon any breach or default of Seller will impair any such right or remedy or be construed to be a waiver of any such breach or default; nor will a waiver of any single breach or default be deemed a waiver of any other breach or default theretofore or thereafter occurring. Any waiver, permit, consent or approval on the part of Purchaser of any breach or default under this Agreement, any Music Rights Schedule or of any provision or condition hereof or thereof, must be in writing specifically set forth.

12

(B) NOTICES. Any notice required or permitted to be given by the provisions hereof must be in writing and will be conclusively deemed to have been received by a party hereto on the day it is delivered to such party at the address indicated below (or at such other address as such party specifies to the other party in writing) or, if sent by registered or certified U.S. mail, on the fifth business day after the day on which mailed, addressed to such party at such address:

MUSIC RIGHTS

If to Seller: _____
                       Street Address, City, State, Zip
                       Attn: _____

If to Purchaser: _____
                       Street Address, City, State, Zip
                       Attn: _____

With a copy to: All parties listed in the Expiration,
                       and License Agreement.

(C) ATTORNEYS' FEES AND COSTS. In the event of any action at law or suit in equity in relation to this Agreement, any Music Rights Schedule, the prevailing party will be entitled to recover from the non-prevailing party attorneys' fees and costs.

(D) APPLICABLE LAW, JURISDICTION AND VENUE. This Agreement and Music Rights Schedule(s) shall be governed by, and construed in accordance with, the laws of the state of California, without regard to principles of conflicts of law. Seller and Purchaser hereby consent to jurisdiction and venue in any state or federal court in the state of California and hereby waive any objections that jurisdiction or venue in any such court is not proper.

(E) SECURITY INTEREST. No security interest in this Agreement, any Music Rights Schedule, may be granted by Seller or Purchaser.

(F) FINANCIAL STATEMENTS. Seller, Assignee agrees to furnish promptly, or cause to be furnished, to the Company within 24 hours of the end of each fiscal quarter, sales statements of Seller prepared in accordance with generally accepted accounting principles, together with such other financial and related information respecting the Seller or the Music Rights as the Company may from time to time reasonably request.

(G) ENTIRE AGREEMENT. Seller and Purchaser acknowledge that there are no agreements or understandings, written or oral, between Seller and Purchaser with respect to the Music Rights and Music Rights Items, other than as set forth herein and in each Music Rights Schedule and that this Agreement and each Music Rights Schedule contain the entire agreement between Seller and Purchaser with respect thereto.

Neither this Agreement, nor any Music Rights Schedule may be altered, modified, terminated or discharged except by the Company in writing to both parties.

13

   (H) SEVERABILITY. Any provision of this Agreement or any Music Rights Schedule prohibited by, or unlawful or unenforceable under, any applicable law in any jurisdiction shall be ineffective as to such jurisdiction without invalidating the remaining provisions of this Agreement; provided, however, that to the extent that the provisions of any such applicable law can be waived, they are hereby waived by Purchaser and Seller.

   (I) NON-SPECIFIED FEATURES. If the Music Rights and Music Rights Items delivered pursuant to any Music Rights Schedule contains any features not specified therein, Purchaser grants Seller, at Seller's option and Seller's expense, the right to remove or deactivate any such features. Such removal or deactivation shall be performed by the Seller or another party reasonably acceptable to Seller, at a time convenient to Purchaser, provided that Purchaser shall not unreasonably delay the removal or deactivation of such features.

   (J) QUIET ENJOYMENT. Provided that no Event of Default has occurred or is continuing hereunder and except as provided herein or in the Maintenance Agreement, Seller, Assignee or their agents or assigns shall not interfere with Purchaser's right of quiet enjoyment and use of the Music Rights and Music Rights Items.

   (K) ALTERATIONS. Purchaser shall not be permitted to make alterations or improvements to the Music Rights.

   (L) HEADINGS. Section headings are for convenience only and shall not be construed as part of this Agreement.

   (M) SUCCESSORS. This Agreement shall inure to and bind the permitted successors and assigns of the respective parties.

   (N) USAGE. In this Agreement the singular includes the plural and the plural the singular. References to agreements and other contractual instruments shall be deemed to include all subsequent amendments and other modifications and supplements thereto, but only to the extent such amendments and other modifications and supplements are not prohibited by the terms of this Agreements. References to any entities include their respective permitted successors and assigns.

(O) FINANCE LEASE STATUS. Purchaser and Seller agree that this Agreement is intended to be a "finance lease" as defined in Article 2A of the UNIFORM COMMERCIAL CODE (or any equivalent state law). PURCHASER WAIVES ANY AND ALL RIGHTS AND REMEDIES CONFERRED UPON A LESSEE BY ARTICLE 2A.

(P) COUNTERPARTS. This Agreement may be signed in several Counterparts in print or electronic form, each of which shall be deemed an original, but all of which shall constitute one and the same instrument.

19. ADDITIONAL DEFINITIONS. The following terms shall have the meanings set forth below:

(A) "CONTRACT YEAR" means each successive twelve (12) calendar month period following the Payment Commencement Date.

14

(B) "FAIR MARKET VALUE" shall mean the in place value of the Music Rights to the Seller and Purchaser/user, as reasonably determined by the Company, which would be obtained in an arms-length transaction between an informed and willing buyer-user under no compulsion to buy and an informed and willing seller under no compulsion to sell, where the expiration and advertising from the places the Music Rights is or will be located pursuant to this Music Rights Schedule during the Term shall not be a deduction from such value. In no event will the Fair Market Value of the Music Rights be less than the original book value.

(C) "INTERIM PAYMENT" means all Lease Payments (as defined in the Music Rights Schedule) from and including the date any Music Rights is activated and listed operational to but excluding the Payment Commencement Date.

(D) "LEASE PAYMENT" has the meaning accorded to such term in the Music Rights Schedule.

(E) "MUSIC RIGHTS ITEMS" means all goods sold and services provided in connection with the Music Rights.

(F) "PAYMENTS" means the Interim Payment, the Lease Payments, as applicable, and all other amounts owed to Purchaser under this Agreement.

(G) "PAYMENT COMMENCEMENT DATE" means the first day of the calendar month immediately following the Acceptance Date.

(H) "PAYMENT DATE" means the first day of each calendar month following the Payment Commencement Date.

(I) "REVENUE" means all sums received by Purchaser or Seller (excluding sales tax actually collected), arising from or in connection with the sale of Merchandise from or usage of the Music Rights.

(J) "SALES REPORTS" means the reports of sales activity of the Music Rights and Music Rights Items generated by computerized sales tracking functions and transmitted to the company or Servicer (if applicable) by modem from Seller.

BY SIGNING THIS AGREEMENT: (1) PURCHASER ACKNOWLEDGES THAT IT HAS READ AND UNDERSTANDS ALL TERMS AND CONDITIONS IN THIS AGREEMENT AND ALL ATTACHMENTS AND EXHIBITS TO THIS AGREEMENT, (2) PURCHASER HAS AN UNCONDITIONAL OBLIGATION TO MAKE ALL PAYMENTS DUE UNDER THIS AGREEMENT, AND THAT PURCHASER CANNOT WITHHOLD, SET-OFF OR REDUCE SUCH PAYMENTS FOR ANY REASON, AND (III) PURCHASER IS LEASING THE MUSIC RIGHTS SOLELY FOR PERSONAL AND OR BUSINESS PURPOSES.

15

IN WITNESS WHEREOF, Seller and Purchaser have caused this Agreement to be duly executed as of the date first above written

Seller: PURCHASER:

Seller   _____   _____
a individual

By: //   _____   By: //_____

Its: Seller   Its: Title

16

Attachment I

M R	National QMS ID	M R Units	M R S	Value	Sales	Unit Price
213	MRQMS2005106X213	1	100	$1.00	N/A	$0.01
901	MRQMS2005106X901	1	100	$1.00	0.65	$0.01
619	MRQMS2005106X619	1	100	$1.00	1.30	$0.01
505	MRQMS2005106X505	1	100	$1.00	0.65	$0.01
406	MRQMS2005106X406	1	100	$1.00	0.60	$0.01

Original M R book value $0.0001

All terms and conditions incorporated in the REVENUE SHARING AND MUSIC RIGHTS
LEASE AGREEMENT DRAFT are attributable to Attachment I Music Rights Schedule.

M R

Authorized Certificate of Units

CERTIFIES the owner of the Unit representing the
total M R minimum Book value $0.0001 U.S.D
per M R of undivided interest. A certified Music
Right, BMI, ASCAP, and Soundscan authorized
encoding. Units held by the Members are
reflected in the electronic Certificate Register of
the Company.

```
M R Certificate of Authenticity 2012
```

M R	National QMS ID	M R Units	M R S	Value	Sales	Unit Price
213	MRQMS2005106X213	1	100	$1.00	N/A	$0.01

Certified Authentication

Differs from Authorized certificate of Units above and are distributed only
by the Authorized Publisher/Provider unless otherwise noted on the MIME Music
Investment and Market Exchange Official market identifier for the national
QMS (Qualified Matching Service) BBS published prices.

Questions

For questions regarding the publisher, content, or published prices please contact or write to:

JMGT Studios Satellite Television Network LLC

7485 SVL Box Victorville, CA 92395

Music Investment and Market Exchange Official market identifier for the national QMS (Qualified Matching Service) BBS published prices

DIGICIRC
MEMORANDUM

ISSN
2166-711X
Issue Price
2.99

National QMS Authorized Publisher

JMGT Studios Satellite Television Network LLC

Address

7485 SVL Box. Victorville, CA 92395

Sub Rights Policy

Purchaser shall have the right to assign this Agreement, any Music Rights Schedule, as a Sublease to the Music Rights without regard to published prices, and any Revenues attributed to the Music Rights.

File No. Not available
ECP

DIGICIRC

MEMORANDUM

Inaugural Issue
Daily

$1.00 U.S.
Inaugural Issue

Sales	Retail	Fee	Value	Outstanding	Value per MR	Increment per sale	Costs	MR Quote
	0.99	0.34	0.65	1	0.65	0.65		
Sales				1				
2			1.3	1	1.3	1.3	0	1.3
3			1.95	1	1.95	1.95	0	1.95
4			2.6	1	2.6	2.6	0	2.6
5			3.25	1	3.25	3.25	0	3.25
6			3.9	1	3.9	3.9	0	3.9
7			4.55	1	4.55	4.55	0	4.55
8			5.2	1	5.2	5.2	0	5.2
9			5.85	1	5.85	5.85	0	5.85
10			6.5	1	6.5	6.5	0	6.5
11			7.15	1	7.15	7.15	0	7.15
12			7.8	1	7.8	7.8	0	7.8
13			8.45	1	8.45	8.45	0	8.45
14			9.1	1	9.1	9.1	0	9.1
15			9.75	1	9.75	9.75	0	9.75
16			10.4	1	10.4	10.4	0	10.4
17			11.05	1	11.05	11.05	0	11.05
18			11.7	1	11.7	11.7	0	11.7
19			12.35	1	12.35	12.35	0	12.35
20			13	1	13	13	0	13
21			13.65	1	13.65	13.65	0	13.65
22			14.3	1	14.3	14.3	0	14.3
23			14.95	1	14.95	14.95	0	14.95
24			15.6	1	15.6	15.6	0	15.6
25			16.25	1	16.25	16.25	0	16.25
26			16.9	1	16.9	16.9	0	16.9
27			17.55	1	17.55	17.55	0	17.55
28			18.2	1	18.2	18.2	0	18.2
29			18.85	1	18.85	18.85	0	18.85
30			19.5	1	19.5	19.5	0	19.5
50			32.5	1	32.5	32.5	0	32.5
60			39	1	39	39	0	39
70			45.5	1	45.5	45.5	0	45.5
100			65	1	65	65	0	65

Baseline Costs

0	per hour	
0	hours	
0		

Sales Trend per quarter

Positive	=	Max Issue	1000	0.25
Negative	=	Min Issue	100	0.25

100   MR   1 unit

Non divided interest

Trade credited to Capital account

with annual distribution to members
Purchase gives the right to be a member. min 2 yr stated
Requirement
2yr agreement waives individual membership
(non active) fee

Individual Membership (non active)
$0.99 Quarterly
$3.96 Annual

Business Membership
$1.99 Quarterly
$7.96 Annual

Artist Membership Monthly per listing
Base rate $0.05per sale

Artist Membership Quarterly per listing
Base rate $0.01per sale

Affiliate membership
$2.99 Quarterly plus Base rate $0.05per sale
$1.99 Quarterly plus Base rate $0.01per sale

$200 Annual

Active participant

Baseline Costs

Sales Trend per quarter

Convert

Individual Membership (active)
$1.29 Quarterly
$5.16 Annual

Forward-looking Statements

The material herein contains forward-looking statements. Such forward-looking statements include, but are not limited to, those related to future earnings, growth and financial and operating performance. Forward-looking statements are not intended to be a guarantee of future results, but instead constitute expectations based on reasonable assumptions. Forecasted financial information is based on certain material assumptions. These assumptions include, but are not limited to, continued normal levels of consumer market purchases, operating performance, as well as achievements of planned productivity improvements and incremental growth.

Actual results could differ materially from those projected in our forward-looking statements due to risks, uncertainties and other factors. Important factors that could affect actual results.

www.ingramcontent.com/pod-product-compliance
Lightning Source LLC
Chambersburg PA
CBHW081307170526
45165CB00011B/3440